Tiny Talks, Big Impact

A Guide to Short Speeches for Busy People

Antoinette Perez

Copyright ©2025 Antoinette Perez
All rights reserved.
ISBN-13: 979-8-9995141-0-3
No portion of this book may be reproduced in any form
without written permission from the publisher or author,
except as permitted by U.S. copyright law.

For Louis

TABLE OF CONTENTS

1. Give a Talk, Move the Needle 11
2. The Tiny Talk Model 23
3. Write Your Tiny Talk 41
4. Practice Your Tiny Talk 61
5. Give Your Tiny Talk 85
6. Receive Feedback on Your Tiny Talk 95
7. Design Your Life, One Tiny Talk at a Time 107
8. Tools + Resources 116

Introduction

I love words. I love letters. I love expression, language, communication, and conversation, and how it all works to build relationships and community. When you think about it, words are the building blocks of our culture and society itself.

In modern times, with attention spans shorter than ever, as well as the demand for words through podcasts and social media video reels, a single person can expand their reach and impact exponentially by translating those written words into spoken form. It only takes a few public speaking skills to go viral with intention.

I've been lucky enough to benefit from an extensive career that's allowed me to play with words, work with words, and shape words, presentations, speeches, and messages that have reached... well, lots of people. (As someone who has developed other speakers, there tends to be an exponential effect to my work that is wild and humbling to watch in action over a long period of time.) I've watched people enraptured by the words of one charismatic and prepared speaker. I've watched people become bored, apathetic, and disengaged by the garbled language of other deeply unserious, less prepared speakers.

I know the power of presentations to inspire, enrage, and heal communities (sometimes in the same speech). I want to help you tap into your own personal power and start adjusting it like a faucet. To be intentional in how you build it, care for it, and use it. To add another exciting tool to your life skills toolbox. Like it or not, this is a world where the right words, spoken to the right audience, at the right time, on the right platform can spark an entire movement. It might be a movement you agree with, but it also might be a movement of hate and division. And the only way to counter it is with words of your own. So get thinking, get writing, and get speaking. The world is counting on you.

What to Expect

I'm going to guess you picked up this book because you have a talk coming up. Maybe it's your first! Maybe you've given a few talks but went with your instinct, don't remember exactly what you said, know it went over ok, and are ready to see what else is out there. I was there once, too. Let me take 30 years of studying public speaking, writing curriculum and creating presentations, and evaluating and coaching speakers, and help you get ready for your next talk.

Are you in a hurry? Go directly to Sections 2-5. They will get you thinking and writing your talk quickly. Come back and read the rest later.

Here are some assumptions I am making:

1. You have been invited or are otherwise expected to talk. That is, you aren't planning to interrupt a wedding, after the officiant has prompted guests to "speak now or forever hold your peace."

2. You expect your audience to be friendly or neutral. This is not a book on how to use a 5-minute talk to achieve conflict resolution. There are hostage negotiation books for that, I hear.

3. You have an hour or two to put your talk together.

I assume that you are here because you are ready to learn a trusted, repeatable way to write a short talk, and then you intend to do it. Depending on how quickly you read, you might expect to read this book in an hour, and then invest another 30 minutes writing your talk. And you could conceivably spend as long as you want practicing, editing, and refining your talk until it's time to give the presentation, but I think 30 more minutes would do it.

How does that sound? Two hours until you have a solid, polished short-form presentation in your hand? Let's get started.

1
GIVE A TALK, MOVE THE NEEDLE

80-20

No talk needs to be perfect. Most of them aren't. We put pressure on ourselves to achieve perfection, but most people don't notice. WE notice, and we assume other people see the imperfection, too. But they usually don't.

For most audiences, the 80-20 rule applies: if 80% of the talk is going well, they're satisfied.

Did I ease your mind? Good.

The 80-20 principle was inspired by 20th-century economist Vilfredo Pareto, who showed that 20% of the population of Italy controlled 80% of the wealth. The tendency of most things is for a small number of factors to cause 80% of outcomes. This "law of disproportionate imbalance" has been observed almost everywhere — in nature (20% of animal populations generate 80% of the offspring in the next generation), in factories (20% of the machines will be responsible for 80% of sellable product), and even in your closet (we wear 20% of our clothes 80% of the time).

And it definitely applies to your talk. Only 20% of all the things you *could* do are going to give you 80% of the results you seek (and probably that 80% satisfaction that your audience wants). This book's job is to whittle down the list of the most important things to focus on, the things that will give you the success you want from your talk.

In the world of tiny talks, this number of things is... tiny.

Conventional wisdom in public speaking suggests a lot of advice that I've found to be incomplete, lacking, or just plain wrong. Here are ten pieces of public speaking advice you're most likely to hear, and what I think you should do instead:

1. Smile and be charming. Exude charisma.

Charisma has value. But in a world of shenanigans and poppycock, with people peddling nonsense dressed up in accepted professional jargon, most audiences prefer authenticity first. After all, if they trust you, they are more likely to trust your message.

2. Memorize your talk, word for word.

Memorizing a talk may result in "dialing in" the presentation, so that you come across robotic and miss connecting with your audience entirely.

3. Don't stumble over your words or forget what you are supposed to say.

Sometimes audiences are distrustful of too much polish in a presentation. Occasionally stumbling over your words, backtracking to cover something you missed, owning up to losing your place in your notes — these feel reassuring for most audiences in small doses, because they see you as a relatable person.

4. Make eye contact with everyone, unless you're too nervous, in which case you should look at a point just above everyone's heads, or imagine the audience naked, or whatever other well-intentioned but ultimately

misleading advice we've gotten about how to calm our nerves.

Making healthy eye contact with people is useful! I've had very intense presenters stare into my eyes like they're hoping to bore a hole through the back of my head. That kind of eye contact isn't great. I've seen presenters focus on that point on the wall just above the audience's eye level, and it looks like they are talking to the wall. Also not good. Making productive eye contact is often a result of good practice. We will get to that.

5. Never turn your back to the audience.

If you're moving and dynamic, you can probably do this without it worrying anyone. Just make sure you don't have your back turned for long, and you aren't doing it to purposely avoid anyone.

6. Only use The Queen's English.

Simple, everyday language makes a speaker feel relatable to an audience.

7. Never use business jargon.

If you're speaking to a business audience and don't use the industry or cultural language, you may be missing out on a chance to connect. The goal is to use language to communicate better, not to obscure what we really mean.

8. Mirror and match your audience.

What if they are dragging and devoid of energy? Do you want to mirror and match that from the stage? I hope not!

Leading a talk means you're leading the room, even if it's only for 5 or 10 minutes. Lead them in the direction of your message.

9. Be polished and appear educated, but not too polished and educated or you'll appear out of touch with your audience.

We're back on that authenticity thing. Be you first. Adjust your delivery during practice.

10. Dress one level above your audience so you can be relatable.

Dress as you will be most comfortable, physically (you can't clip a microphone battery pack on a dress with no belt), as well as mentally (would you rather fit in? If not, how do you want to stand out, and how much?).

If any of these tips have worked for you, ignore me and keep doing it because everyone's style is different. (Except the advice to "imagine your audience naked." Stop that right now. It's creepy.) But if you also found any of this advice puzzling, confusing, and inconsistent, feel free to drop it immediately.

Soon you'll have the tools and guidance to write your own Tiny Talk, and you'll be on your way to deciding whether you're ready to open doors for yourself and remake your very identity. I hope you will.

The clock is ticking! So let's get to it.

Head + Heart + Hands

Think about the talks that have moved you, stirred something inside you. What parts of you were activated during and even after the talks?

A successful, memorable talk creates an experience by engaging and activating an audience in three ways:

HEAD

A good talk will get the audience's minds working, the gray matter thinking, the mental gears grinding. The audience may be hearing new ideas, or putting familiar ideas together in new ways. They may hear a phrase that challenges long-held assumptions and yet rings true. They are fully engaged in the excitement and energy of ideas and thoughts.

For many audiences, the first point of activation is the head.

HEART

A good talk will stir emotions. Don't be intimidated by this. Stirring emotions means that what you are saying is landing for your audience in a meaningful way. If you've also activated their brains, they are connecting the dots between your ideas and outcomes they may experience. You're connecting with them emotionally.

If we don't write a talk that ignites both the head and the heart — if we only offer tantalizing brain nuggets (data, information, statistics, facts), we are missing a level of connection, as well as the opportunity to take the ideas we are sharing into the physical world in the form of action. It's imperative that we make meaning of the information we are sharing, and reach for that new dimension of connecting with our audience emotionally.

Here's an example of the limits of good ideas that most of us have experienced: How many of us have known that we need to eat better and exercise more, and yet we still eat chips, drink soda, and skip the gym most days? Then we hear that someone we went to college with has had a health scare due to their poor eating and low activity levels, and suddenly we're taking wheatgrass shots and jumping on boxes with a crossfit trainer. We can know something in our heads, yet until that thing is known in our hearts, our understanding is limited.

HANDS

A good talk may even inspire the audience to new or different actions. Left to their own devices, people hearing the right message at the right time will take action afterwards, because they will continue to connect the ideas from your talk to potential actions and results that could occur.

You can take a more direct approach to action by closing your talk with a to-do, a "homework assignment," or a challenge — in the sales world this is known as a "call to action." This is a purposeful way to address those in the room who have been waiting for a push, and lucky for them, you showed up today.

The Tiny Talk Model will show you how to create this "whole body experience" for your audience by engaging their heads, hearts, and hands, in a 5-10 minute talk.

True Tiny Talk: Brittany

Brittany came to my two-day Train the Trainer workshop. She was high-strung from the get-go. On the first day, everyone would learn the presenting models and build a 10-minute presentation with them. On the second day, everyone would stand up and deliver their presentation for feedback and evaluation.

Brittany didn't participate much in class discussions on the first day, but it was clear from her copious notes that she soaked up everything she heard. When Brittany walked to the front of the room to deliver her presentation, she was visibly shaking. Armed with a thick stack of index cards upon which she had written her entire presentation word for word, Brittany's voice shook as well.

Her message wasn't bad. It was clear that Brittany had knowledge of her subject and knew the words she wanted to use. But her delivery distracted from any clarity or power in the message. She was unwilling to let go of any control, essentially choking the life out of her own presentation by controlling every single word she said. She was dedicated to the purity of her message, at the cost of nothing resonating or retained by her audience.

I've watched thousands of these short-form presentations, and one thing I know is that context matters for each presenter. Brittany confirmed that this was the first time she had given a formal presentation in her life. And so my feedback considered this: I suggested that she present more often, so that she could start to tackle the obvious nerves and begin to trust herself. I asked her to write fewer words on her notes, so she would force herself to rely on her conversational ability rather than a script. And I suggested she simplify her central message so that she could repeat it several times until it became a mantra for her audience.

All I could remember a year later, seeing her name on the roster for Advanced Workshop, was watching the top of her head for 10 full minutes the year prior.

Imagine my surprise when Brittany walked to the front of the room this time, with no notes, making full eye contact, asking engaging open questions of the group, and expertly guiding the discussion to hit all her learning goals. Everyone agreed that she gave the most memorable and valuable presentation of the day.

I asked her what she had done to improve so much from the year before. She said that, recognizing how anxious she had been, she volunteered to give a presentation each week at her team meeting. She also signed up to facilitate a monthly group mastermind which she'd only attended before. In other words, she intentionally pushed herself outside her comfort zone to step up to roles of higher visibility, and she committed to doing the work to prepare for each event, gather feedback, and learn from it. Over time, she built her confidence, her sense of style, and her command of a room. She was literally not the same person she had been just one year prior.

On a break, I heard a little more context from her regional director: not only had Brittany's presentation skills improved, but her enhanced skill set of preparation, curiosity, drive, and inclusion had made her a go-to resource at work long after the meetings were over. She was leading effectively, and earning a reputation as a strong leader.

What I was treated to was yet another demonstration of the value of Tiny Talks. I've seen many such examples in my 20-year career coaching public speakers and facilitators. It doesn't take much to go from a bundle of nerves at the front of the room to a strong presence that instills trust. You could spend a lot of time and money to improve as a public speaker, but you don't have to. All you need to know are personal areas of improvement, and a commitment to work on them.

Your Coffee Shop Barista Doesn't Need a Speech -- But Your Work Team Might

As we interact with people around us on a daily basis, we talk a lot. We have a lot of conversations. Some take mere seconds. Most are spontaneous. To be sure, not every conversation needs to be thought through, prepared for, and shaped. Nor do we want every conversation to be completely one-sided. Part of the beauty of conversation is co-creating it, and building relationships through it.

But when you have an occasion that warrants a Tiny Talk, do the work. At first it will seem like just that — work. But the more you use the Tiny Talk model, the more natural it will feel. Eventually it will just be one way you construct short-form presentations on the fly.

I'm going to share with you the essential components of a great Tiny Talk, and then it's up to you to decide if you want to do the work.

The Tiny Talk Model is great when:
1. The outcome matters to you — you have a vested interest in the success of the talk.
2. You have something to say! You want to deliver a message.
3. You want the audience to think or act differently.

At work, your boss may ask you to
- Present a new project, product, or program — or give updates to those already progressing.
- Share a trend that's shifting business for your company.
- Give updates on topics and issues adjacent to your work.

You may get invited to speak at a conference to offer
- A new idea in your specialization.

- A succinct deep dive into your area of expertise.

Friends, family, and co-workers will ask you to
- Give a toast at a wedding.
- Say a few words about a retiring colleague.
- Offer reflections about a deceased loved one.

Even now, you might be resisting this request for you to prepare a talk:
- "I don't like the spotlight!"
- "I am not the right person for this!"
- "So-and-so is the performer, not me! Why didn't they ask them to give a speech?"

Someone believes you have something to say that is worth other people hearing. They believe you have a unique point of view or an opportunity to change the way people think or behave. That is why you've been invited to speak. Ultimately, this talk isn't about you at all – it's about other people.

So brush off the feelings that are holding you back or slowing you down, and let's get you ready to deliver a brief but powerful talk that you will be proud of.

2
THE TINY TALK MODEL

The Tiny Talk Model

Tiny Talks are:

- Purposeful — Know why you're giving the talk, and write your talk to fulfill the why.

- Prepared — A tiny bit of forethought can mean the difference between merely saying a bunch of words / taking up airspace and delivering a message that lands.

- Practiced, if we have time — Ironically, people obsess most over their amount of polish, but tend to skip this step.

Tiny Talks represent a sweet spot that resides at the intersection of three things:

1. You (who you are);

2. Your message (what you want to say);

3. Your audience (how you want them to feel, and a bonus that really puts the cherry on top: what we want them to do after the talk).

THE TINY TALK MODEL.

Let's dig into these three components a little further.

You (Who You Are)

You are the author and performer, and for 5-10 minutes, you will command the stage. You will start out as the center of attention. But if you do your job right, you will shift the audience's attention quickly so that the message becomes the focus. You'll be a messenger, delivering a message in service of your audience.

This is not to say that we need to talk about ourselves during our Tiny Talk. In fact, most of the time it's better if we *don't* center ourselves during our Tiny Talk. (Exception: If we have been asked to share a personal story for an audience that is related to a change we propose. Even then, we should tell our story *in service of* a message — not as a replacement of the message. More on that later.)

It's OK if you do like attention! You'll get that anyway. Who we are will show up whether we speak to it directly or not. So we should be aware that the words and phrases we choose, the energy and focus we bring, even how we physically appear can all affect the message we're working so hard to craft.

For the Tiny Talk model, the message must be centered. How you write and deliver your talk can garner attention, but if your audience misses the message, you missed the mark. You getting attention should be a byproduct of delivering a great message that connects with your audience.

Speakers commonly sidetrack themselves right off the top of their talk, in their introduction. They worry too much about establishing credibility for their audience, so they list every title they've earned, going back to their scouting days, as well as all the processional accreditations, certifications, and resume builders. And they begin their talk on the offense, by preemptively lobbing it all at the audience before anyone has a chance to question their expertise.

Remember that the audience is almost always more interested in how you are related to the thing you're talking about than your specific credentials.

Sometimes credentials are important and relevant. In certain situations, like a pitch meeting to a cross-departmental team for a potential project, your audience may decide whether or not to listen based on how much experience you have managing this type of project. But in other situations, such as a wedding toast, the audience is probably more interested in how you are related to the bride and groom than how many previous toasts you've given.

Consider two core questions:

1. What is the least amount of information about yourself you can convey to this audience to earn their trust for the next few minutes?

You aren't trying to withhold information due to bad intent — you are respecting your audience's time and attention span by planning thoughtfully what is most important for them to know about you at the start of your talk. (After earning their trust so they willingly pay attention for a bit, you can plant another bit of information about yourself to hook them and earn their trust again, for another minute or two. And you'll repeat this to the end of your talk.)

Also keep in mind that as you talk, the stories you tell, and how you present your ideas will reveal more about you for your audience, without requiring you to list your resume and qualifications. And as you reveal more about yourself in an authentic way, you earn more trust and more time with your audience.

2. What is at the heart of your relationship to the people, project, or occasion you're speaking of? What context is helpful for the audience to have about you and the thing you're talking about?

I've been to weddings where a person rises to give a toast to the bride and groom, and they don't introduce themselves. From the content of their talk, I have to start piecing together who they are, and their relationship to the happy couple. As a listener, I'm doing way too much mental labor in this talk, and I may be working so intently on figuring out who you are that I miss other parts of your talk that are actually meaningful, like your message.

While not revealing your entire context can be a fun way to set up your talk, it should be intentional and not the result of poor writing on your part. Let your audience focus on your message instead of stitching together tangential elements of your talk.

A Humble Request

Please do not write a talk to deliver to an audience just to hear yourself speak. There are other suitable platforms for people who want to have something to say, but haven't done the work to connect their message to their audience. Podcasts, for instance, are a popular medium with a low barrier to entry for anyone with a smartphone and words to speak. Talks with a live audience are a meaningful opportunity to help people think and do differently. Accept this responsibility by accepting that you are the conduit and the message is the star of the show.

Your Message (What You Want to Say)

This is the point! The person who invited you to speak believes that the message you have inside you is worth shushing everyone for 5-10 minutes to listen to you. They are interested in your message, from your specific point of view. They believe you have something uniquely valuable to say. So invest some time and brain power to craft a tiny talk that packs a punch.

If you're fuzzy about your message, it will show. You'll add too many words. Sometimes, your first explanation will not jibe with your second explanation. When you ask three separate people after the talk what they understood as the main takeaway, they will tell you three different things.

Think of your message as a rally or battle cry. What single sentence encapsulates the point of your talk?

No two creative processes are the same, but I've found that if I can articulate the central idea of a talk before I do anything else, I'll have an easier time writing and eventually editing (and refocusing) the talk.

Or maybe you have a creative process that requires you to dump out all the thoughts in your brain, and make sense of them visually, editing down to that one sentence that is your message. Great, do that.

I'm not suggesting that any of the following iconic and well-known talks should be reduced to one sentence. But after listening to each, we can clearly understand that they revolve around one central message.

Martin Luther King: I Have A Dream (1963)

The time for America to make good on its promise of democracy, justice, and freedom to ALL Americans, even Black Americans, is now.

Steve Jobs: MacWorld Conference iPhone Reveal (2007)

Thank you to our users, who have supported our company with enthusiastic purchases. We made something new for you that can combine almost everything you enjoy now: photos, music, movies, email, internet, gaming, and – oh yeah, a phone – into one device. It's called the iPhone and now we are going to save you from buying all those individual devices and price the iPhone starting at $499.

Chimamanda Ngozi Adichie: We Should All Be Feminists (2011)

(I don't really need to summarize this talk in one sentence because she did it in the title! Masterful. But here's a little more detail.) A feminist believes gender inequality exists, commits to fixing it, and then takes action to fix it, in themselves and in how they raise the next generation of humans.

On the flip side, here are a couple of examples of too-wordy messages and how you can make them strong and concise.

Example #1: Post-product release debrief, in a team meeting

Too wordy: To be sure, this project was not perfect. What project ever is? Our own company has never released a product that received a 100% satisfaction rating, so I'm not ashamed of our early numbers, posting an 88% client satisfaction rating. In fact, our company's highest rating ever, prior to now, was 84% and the average among all products is 72%. As a company we are doing better than the industry average, which is 67%. Of course we can improve, and we will.

Concise: This product was our company's strongest ever with an 88% client satisfaction rating, and of course there is room to improve. We are proud *and* we will take the client feedback and incorporate it into the next release.

Example #2: Asking an executive sponsor at your company for funding for a new project

Too wordy: I'm sure you are wondering what kind of budget I'm suggesting for this. It's hard to say, because there are so many variables that could affect going big or going small. It depends on the quality of the prototype you want, how full-featured it is. We could keep the price tag lower if you could assign more internal resources, say if we had six team members dedicating 5 hours a week to this project. The budget could get really big if you decided we could contract some resources for this, maybe from the same company we used last year. I don't know if they're available. But if they are, they could send in a consultant and we could hit the finish line relatively quickly with something you might be proud to share with the executive team. I could see that ballooning to $250,000 pretty quickly. If we stayed internal for prototype development, and we absolutely had to, we can probably do this on the cheap for $100,000.

Concise: There are many factors we can control that will affect the budget. I'm confident that we can produce a prototype for $100,000, but we will be able to deliver on more features and with a higher build quality at $250,000.

The simpler our message, the better. Simplicity gives us clarity, and clarity is power.

Your Audience (How You Want Them to Feel)

Your audience is the group of people who will receive your talk. You may have a guest of honor who is the subject of your talk, in which case your primary audience is that person and the secondary audience is everyone else. The ultimate measure of success for your talk is how well your audience responds to and retains your message.

Your choice of words and phrases will do a lot to set a tone for your talk. So before you write a single word of your talk, it's worthwhile to ask how you want them to feel during your talk.
- If you're getting a team ready to take on a new challenge, do you want them to feel energized and resilient?
- If you're delivering remarks at a loved one's eulogy, do you want the audience to feel inspired by this honored person's life?
- If you're introducing a new team member, do you want your audience to feel warm and welcoming?

If it helps, imagine the faces of people as they are experiencing your talk. Are their looks hopeful? Motivated? Wondrous? The more precisely you can identify how you want your audience to feel, the more purposeful your words and phrases will be to create that environment.

A Brief Note on Feelings in the Workplace

As a person who's comfortable with the full range of human emotion, and who has had a strong need to express myself since I was able to communicate, it's still surprising to me how many people are uncomfortable discussing and experiencing emotions in general, especially at work. I'm not sure where the misconception originated that human beings would be able to put their very human emotions in a box and leave them at home for weeks or longer at a time. Heaven forbid we bring our human emotions into the workplace. Somewhere along the way, we started equating non-emotionality in the workplace with professionalism.

Let me explain. Some workplaces dismiss and reject "negative" emotions. You might work in a company where no one has *problems*, because *problems* feel "negative". Everyone has been trained to speak instead of *challenges*, a "positive" word that carries the connotation of grit and perseverance. Charming reframe! But if we wave the positivity wand at everything, all the time, we create a culture of imprecise and inaccurate language. And because everything we say is coded with a "positive" slant, we might obscure the very facts, truth, and reality that we need to find long-term, sustainable solutions. Let's lead the way to better decisions and outcomes by welcoming back all the feelings.

Emotions drive our decisions, and eventually our actions. This is the human condition. The more emotions we can acknowledge, the more action we can inspire. When we talk, even for 5 minutes, we have an opportunity to invite people to feel a certain way about the idea we're proposing, the program we are pitching, the change in direction the project needs to go to stay on deadline.

And when you think about it, if you don't care about how your audience feels after your talk, why bother giving a talk at all? You can email data and charts and statistics and save everyone the pain of yet another meeting. Of course offering a talk gives you a chance to frame the data, charts, and statistics with context and deeper understanding. It allows you to curate all that someone could know about a topic into the most important things they should know, acknowledging what they might feel, and suggesting an action they should take because of that. You're leading them.

Set the Tone for How You Want Your Audience to Feel

Figuring out what you want your audience to feel is a great way to drill down on the tone you want to create for your talk. Tone will help you decide the words and phrases that will best communicate your message. Tone will offer a chance for consistency between your talk (cause) and how your audience thinks about your talk, and what they do with it (effect).

Two brief examples of emotions and tone / word choice:

Message: Question everything.
We can strike different tones by using different phrases. "Don't let anyone tell you that your POV as a young person

is naive," could be encouraging, while, "Don't let older generations gaslight you into believing that your questions and ideas aren't valuable," feels like it stirs the pot a bit.

Message: Push past complacency in mid-career.

There's a big difference between, "You deserved a break, and now your team is ready for you to lead them into the ring for round 2" (sympathetic) and, "Your community is counting on you to apply everything you have learned as a successful businessperson for the benefit of generations to come" (aspirational).

Your Audience (What You Want Them to Do)

Remember, this step is optional. A lot of great, solid, short-form talks never ask a thing of their audience, and they receive appreciation and accolades all the same. If you can find the sweet spot between who you are, the message you want to deliver, and how you want your audience to feel, and say it in 5-10 minutes, you will no doubt have accomplished a lot. There is a bonus element to a tiny talk that you don't *have* to achieve — but if you do, you may hear about your talk for years to come.

Self-help and personal and professional development spaces are brimming with promises of "transformation." The premise is that if you attend a personal development seminar, or read a self-help book, you should emerge transformed. The seller of the self-help is promising you transformation if you just take the seminar or buy the book, because their ideas and systems are *just that good*.

Maybe their ideas and systems have transformational potential. The flaw, though: transformation is not the job of the person sharing the ideas and information, nor is it the job of the ideas and information themselves. Transformation is up to the person *receiving* the ideas and information. There's a big step that isn't acknowledged in this logic that the person learning new things needs to try those things. There's a difference between knowing and doing. And the transformation is never in the knowing, but always in the doing.

While five minutes isn't enough time for most of us to transform, it's definitely enough time for a seed to be planted, and a challenge issued for someone to take action. And that first step might be *the* thing someone needs to begin their journey of transformation.

At the end of your talk, ask yourself whether your audience now knows enough to take some new or different action, based on what you covered:

• If you gave a speech for a co-worker's retirement, sharing that they always saw the best in everyone, ask everyone at the end of your talk to talk with at least three people on their way out of the room, and tell them one thing they appreciate about them.
• If you toasted the 40-year-old birthday boy's warm hugs, invite your audience to celebrate this birthday by giving him a big hug before the night is over.

- If you honored a friend's life by spotlighting their ability to nurture deep friendships, challenge your audience to call a friend they haven't spoken with in a while, to rekindle and nurture that mutual friend that you will all miss.

I think you get the picture. Think of an action that your audience can do to take the message from your talk and extend it into real life. This is very much the proverbial cherry on top, but can elevate any talk from a good idea to an effective action.

Remember that a successful, memorable talk engages head + heart + hands. Plenty of talks make a difference and only cover the first two. Most TED talks are limited to engaging head and heart, by design (its byline is "ideas worth spreading," not "actions worth taking"), so please don't think that a talk that only does those two things is a talk not worth giving.

But this final step of engaging "hands", aka getting your audience to take immediate action on your idea, can truly change the way people think, behave, and act on an ongoing basis.

If you are able to not just communicate a strong message to your audience, but invite them to take an action that gives that idea physical form, they may trust you enough to do it. And, not to put pressure on you, but it might change something real for them that they will never forget.

Mental Organization Worksheet

Now it's time to get mentally organized for your tiny talk.

Using a random sheet of paper or the Mental Organization Worksheet in the RESOURCES section at the back of this book, write one sentence or a few phrases in response to each prompt.

1. Who are you?

Share information your audience may not know and will find helpful as they listen to your talk.

How are you related to the topic / guest of the day? If appropriate, connect some dots for your audience about how you are related to the topic, guest, or overall message.

2. What is your message?

Narrow this down to one sentence or phrase. This is the key take-away from your talk. If someone asked your audience afterward what your talk was about, this is the one sentence response they would give. Be concise and succinct.

I've found that this can be very difficult for me to articulate in one concise sentence. And that's usually because I'm worried about nuance, and shades of grey, and fairness and balance. Sometimes it's because I'm afraid of the strength of my own voice. Write what first comes to mind, and then see if you can simplify it to its absolute essence.

Worry about nuance and detail later. For now, you're the only one to see this, so let yourself be true to you.

An example thought progression might look like this:

"I want everyone to commit to being more emotionally intelligent so we can be a more effective world community." —> "Our world will be better if we are each committed to being better for the world." —> "Be a better human."

3. Who is your audience?

How are *they* related to the topic / guest / message?

How do you want them to feel during this talk? Use adjectives! Instead of, "I want them to feel like they can take over the world," list, "emboldened, powerful, energized".

What do you want them to do after your talk?
This is optional, but if you already know one action you'd be thrilled for each audience member to take that was a direct result of your talk, put it here.

3
WRITE YOUR TINY TALK

Write Your Tiny Talk

The act of writing is fundamentally a creative process. And creative processes are very personal. What works for me won't necessarily work with the same results for you.

But in the Tiny Talk Template I'm about to share with you, I've built in one choice I believe is best for nearly every short-form presentation: when faced with choosing between depth or breadth during a talk, I almost always go for depth.

In other words, if you only have 5 or 10 minutes, I suggest going deep and not wide. What seems to most emotionally resonate with an audience is to choose one idea, as opposed to the brain tickle you can sometimes elicit from brushing up against several ideas that only get a minute or two each.

Let's say that in five minutes, we have an option for a talk about one idea that includes one story, one data point, and a few thought-provoking questions. I would have a reasonable chance of shifting some of our audience's thinking. The second option is to spend our entire five minutes providing three data points on three topics – but then we miss our chance to access emotions (through story) and encourage self-discovery (through questions). We might reach the data folks among the audience but possibly no one else.

Think about a time when you listened to a 10-minute talk and the speaker covered a lot of topics. You may have heard a range of ideas, but you probably didn't understand them thoroughly or learn enough about them to apply them. You may not have even remembered all the main points of the presentation after the talk was over.

By contrast, think of a 10-minute talk you heard that covered only one idea. The speaker explored that topic from multiple perspectives. You probably got a variety of senses involved and were able to access some emotional connection to the topic. As a result, you retained more and might even have been moved enough to take action.

The 5-minute template is designed to cover only one topic, but to go deep into it. The 10-minute template allows up to 3 topics, but even that is pushing the boundaries of what you can cover well in that amount of time. I have a strong bias toward talks going deep rather than staying on the surface, so even if you have 10 minutes, consider prioritizing one topic and two only if you must.

If you want your talk to be 5 minutes or less, your word count should be about 750 words. If you have up to 10 minutes for your talk, you could expect to speak 1,500 words in that time.

Without practicing right this second, you can use the rule of thumb of 150 words per minute to estimate the length of your talk. Don't worry if you seem to be far above or below. If the talk is complete, it's complete. Practice, which we will cover in the next chapter, will give you the next critical checkpoint for timing and a more solid sense of your personal average word count per minute.

After writing the first draft of your Tiny Talk, I recommend that you take only one pass at editing. This is because nearly everyone — new speakers and very experienced speakers alike — puts off the very first practice session. And one easy place to procrastinate is to keep editing the talk on paper / on the screen: putting a story in a different place; moving a joke from the start to the finish; endlessly tinkering with phrasing until it looks perfect.

At a certain point, the constant editing will not help you make decisions, and you will probably start to feel the heavy weight of indecision. In fact, it may be hurting your ability to make good choices, because you are overwhelming your brain with options.

Write your talk. Edit it one time. Stop where you are, take a break, and come back to your talk later to practice.

And remember the formula:

Head + Heart + Hands = Tiny Talk Total Experience

• *Head = data, charts, graphs, numbers, graphics, metaphors, questions*

• *Heart = photos, stories, humor, questions, references for relatability, metaphors, questions*

• *Hands = call to action, challenge, try something new / different*

Now let's take a look at some specific elements, or types of content, you can include in your talk.

Data

How much data should you include in your talk? A persuasive talk may be helped by one simple yet compelling data point, even if the setting for your talk is personal. If you're giving a work presentation, you may be especially tempted to load your presentation with as much data as possible.

Regardless of whether your talk is personal or professional, I recommend that you consider, out of all the data you could include, only 1-3 points that offer the most compelling perspective for your talk.

Only include one point if your talk is 5 minutes; you could try to include up to three points for a 10-minute talk, but that's ambitious for most people.

One of the biggest risks of presenting data is the possibility that you are offering a distraction, not focus. For some people, data may offer an interesting mental side road for them to take while you have moved onto your next point. For one person, this data could be a point of disagreement that they will (hopefully) wait to bring up after the talk. Be very judicious that you aren't cherry picking data that someone might find problematic. And above all, be confident that the data point will be more of an asset to your talk than a risk.

If you decide to use data, you can acknowledge your data selection with a quick statement, like: "There is a lot of research on this topic, and I can share a list of other resources with you later. In the spirit of keeping this presentation brief, I've settled on one data point that frames our project better than any other."

Humor

If humor is not natural for you, the time to manufacture it is not now, during your Tiny Talk.

However, I have good news. You don't have to have jokes to bring humor to your talk.

Long ago, as a newer public speaker, I attended a session with a very experienced speaker who implored us to stop trying to *be funny*, and instead to *find the funny*.

This advice clicked with me immediately. I've always felt kinship with silliness. Growing up as a kid, watching Looney Tunes every Saturday morning, I saw parallels between my real life and the cartoon world. Cartoons were simply exaggerations of emotions and situations that had real life origins or significance. Even now, at age 50, I experience quite a bit of life as though it's a cartoon, fodder for poking fun at ourselves and enjoying a little outlandish satire.

So don't pressure yourself to make things funny — just dial into what's already making you laugh, and describe it.

The good news is that you can practice the funny parts of your talk and improve them, or drop them for now.

Talking about humorous experiences can make us and our talk relatable. Sharing a humorous story or even telling a short joke that elicits a chuckle can create a lightheartedness that we may want to balance heavier themes in our talk. Aiming to create a laugh-out-loud moment can really pay off by changing the energy in the room in an instant, and allows us to possibly switch tones entirely for the rest of our talk.

One quality to use sparingly, if you use it at all, is self-deprecation. Self-deprecating humor lets you poke fun at yourself, for the benefit of the audience and the talk. Self-deprecation can help take the edge off a very strong, dominant personality, and can make us feel more familiar if we aren't well known to the audience. Taken too far, self-deprecation can make an audience uncomfortable, turn things awkward and occasionally center the speaker themselves in the talk instead of the message.

Metaphors

Metaphors can work wonders for a talk. Metaphors allow people to relate to your message using an experience they already know. The good news is that metaphors abound. You don't need to stick to your industry to find a good metaphor to serve your talk and your audience.

Having said that, here are some rules-of-thumb for effective metaphors.

1. Understandable

In order for a metaphor to be effective, the audience needs to understand how that thing they already know is related to the thing you're telling them. This may require some explanation. It also means that if you love metaphors and think in metaphor all the time, you may be better served focusing on one central metaphor through your talk, instead of using many metaphors and requiring as much mental work from your audience.

2. Relatable

A metaphor will be a winner if most or all people in the room can relate to it. If you use parenting as a metaphor with a room of 20-somethings, you may find that they understand the metaphor intellectually, but not emotionally.

Sometimes, when I talk with a group about a new skill and the importance of doing daily "drills" of the fundamentals, I will bring them back to school days by saying, "If you played team sports as a kid, you remember doing drills on the soccer field to improve your aim at corner kicks, or changing direction 180 degrees on a basketball court. If you were a music kid, you remember singing or playing scales as a warm-up each day. Same idea."

3. Right-sized

If you haven't guessed, I am a metaphor user. And abuser! I will stretch a metaphor until it's become a caricature. Until I've reached to the next solar system for parallels. Until a metaphor is an empty husk of itself. I don't know why I do this, but don't be me. Use your metaphor, make your point, and get out.

4. Visual

As mentioned earlier, you can reach outside of your industry or topic to grab a compelling metaphor. Nature has a great way of showing up, even in structure or form, in all the things we do. Don't shy away from calling on a visual to draw a parallel to your topic, possibly even bringing in a sample as a visual prop. (And yes, you can use a slide for this if it's helpful and you have the technology.)

Questions

In a short-form presentation, you could plan no questions of your audience at all, and it's likely no one would realize it. Which is another way of saying if you don't have to ask questions, then don't.

But some audiences, especially work audiences, appreciate being included, or invited to participate, even if minimally.

Here are three effective ways to use questions in your Tiny Talk.

1. The closed question disguised as an open question

If you want to invite quick spoken responses from your audience, ask a closed question disguised as an open question. This is a question that you will likely ask toward the front of your talk that helps set the stage by establishing common ground. It is a question that feels like there could be an infinite number of responses, but really there will be at most three responses that a hundred people would give over and over. A successful closed question disguised as an open question can add a lot of pep and engagement to a talk.

2. The rhetorical question

If you want your audience to feel pensive and thoughtful, asking one or two rhetorical questions can focus their thinking very quickly. This is usually a question you expect them to answer in their heads, like, "Wouldn't it be great to live in a world where you could be completely yourself, all the time?" It's useful to think about how to set up the question before you ask it, so that they understand the importance of answering the question for themselves, and the stakes if they don't.

Silent self-discovery allows every audience member to answer a rhetorical question and grow at their own pace. Some people are ready to be unlocked, and your rhetorical question may be the key they've been waiting for. You'll know this has happened after you give a ten-minute talk to a hundred people, and a year later someone emails you and says, "Your talk last year changed my life." What they mean is, something you said or asked helped them unlock something that they used to change their own life! Head + heart + hands in action!

3. A call-and-response

If you're talking before a lively group and audience interaction is welcome or even expected, there may be a key phrase you can introduce early that is a theme or "lesson learned" for your talk. Over time, as you repeat the phrase, you can add a pause before saying it, gesture to the group that they should say it along, and eventually get to the point where you can ask a question, give them a signal, and let them fill in the blank. Some comedians do this to great effect in their stand-up routines, and you can do it, too. This is one way to raise energy and introduce humor without having to tell jokes.

Relatability via Common References

Sharing a common reference is one way to team up with an audience and get everyone feeling like you're all on the same team.

"Isn't it funny how we grew up on devices plugged into walls (TV's, phones) and now we routinely operate at any given moment by multitasking between several wireless devices at once?"

"Don't you love it when you have five minutes to call your doctor's office to resolve a billing error, and the first thing you hear on the other end of the line is a recorded voice, welcoming you into the dark underbelly of interactive voice response?"

"Who are these people who 'run marathons for fun'? I find nothing fun about running to the end of my block, much less 26 miles. I don't even like *driving* 26 miles!"

A common reference shows your audience that you are someone just like them. It builds trust quickly, which deepens engagement with you and receptiveness to your message.

Avoid polarizing references. You don't want to alienate people in your audience.

The marathon reference seems, on the surface, as though it may be polarizing. But it should be clear from your words, tone of voice, and facial expressions that you are not literally disparaging people who run marathons, but they are triggering feelings in you of underachievement, or envy, or some other exaggerated emotion, because of these athletes' excellence. This is an interesting way of presenting a reference that seems to divide the room but in fact you're acknowledging both sides as valid.

Political references are the most obvious polarizing references you could choose and should avoid — unless you know your audience is a political audience, comprised of people who share the same beliefs.

A common reference that everyone can relate to or rally around is a quick path to solidarity and quickly getting your audience on message.

Hot tip: Don't be afraid to capture attention quickly by opening with an "unpopular opinion." Bonus points if it's amusing as well.

An unpopular opinion will engage people quickly and deeply, as they consider whether they have an opinion of their own. They will usually give your talk a fair shake if they haven't yet decided.

Similar to common references, ask yourself whether your unpopular opinion is polarizing, and whether the engagement and intrigue that your unpopular opinion generates outweighs the possibility that someone in the audience will feel turned off by the strength of your opinion.

Slides

Don't.

Don't use slides unless you're giving a work presentation and there's one critical visual that you absolutely must share. Even in this case, I recommend you consider instead distributing a copy for each person instead of relying on a slide.

Don't use slides unless you're presenting at a Pecha Kucha night. But you're reading the wrong book for that.

Don't use slides unless you are roasting someone at their birthday party and have photographs aka evidence for the ages. Then you absolutely must use slides.

Why am I so anti-slide? For a few reasons.

- We can get very dependent on slides. All too often, there's miscommunication and someone forgets to bring a computer to run the slide show. Or the technology won't talk to each other. Or (this has happened to me and I hated it) the projection is so small that you have it, but most people can't see it well, and you've wrapped your talk around everyone being able to see the slide.

- Slides can distract from you and your message. If you're shy, maybe you think that's the point. You would rather everyone not focus solely on you. Just remember you have a message to deliver. You are not the focus. The message is. And if people are too distracted by the slide, they may miss what you have to say entirely.

- Finally, I have again fallen into this trap of working to make the slide and the visual perfect. It's another way we can get stuck in preparation and never get to the practicing of our talk. And we must always practice our talk! (Next chapter.)

So, my advice is: keep things simple. If there's no requirement to use slides, don't.

Stories

Unsurprisingly, stories may comprise most of your talk. In my experience, story usually plays an important role in casual short-form presentations.

But even presentations at work can benefit from one succinct but entirely relevant story to help you illustrate your message. Usually you want this story to personalize the situation, help your audience consider a different point of view, and maybe even make an entire group more relatable to your audience.

Especially at work, be sure that every story you tell is true. Any customer avatars or client profiles should be prefaced as such, or introduced as "fictional case studies" — those are not stories as I'm addressing them now.

Here are two paths to writing your story. Pick the one that gives you the most creative drive:

1. Write your story as briefly as possible, later adding the details that seem most helpful for creating the tone and experience you want.

2. Or write down every single character, setting change, and plot twist, and make choices later about the extraneous details you will cut.

Don't confuse a story with a platitude or truth, a fact, an example, or an anecdote. Or a metaphor! An example:

Platitude: Don't wait until you're old to start living: life is too short to postpone your happiness.

Truth: Many people dream of traveling in their retirement years, despite fearing they won't have enough money or the good health to travel.

Fact: According to a November 2021 Transamerica Center for Retirement Studies survey, traveling is the most common activity people dream of doing after they stop working - 65% - though 42% of the same respondents fear they will outlive their savings and investments.

Anecdote: My friends Ellie and Carl worked hard to save for their "vacation of a lifetime" but sadly, Ellie didn't live long enough to enjoy it.

Story: Ellie and Carl grew up together, got married, and dreamed of traveling to South America in retirement. Tragically, Ellie passed away before they had the means to do so. After a period of seclusion and development into a full-blown curmudgeon, 78-year-old Carl took the least expensive path to South America on his own by tying helium balloons to his house and navigating his way there. He ended up with unexpected stowaways and picked up some exotic wildlife along the way. Through their adventures, Carl is reminded that caring for others, and being cared for, gives life and all its surprises meaning, purpose, and joy.

And you absolutely must promise not to mislead your audience by turning a meme, urban legend, myth, or generalized story you read on the internet into a story. In the early days of email, older generations would send each other "chain emails" with generic motivational graphics and various morality tales dressed up in more modern clothes. Of course, these older generations would occasionally exercise their "forwarding" muscles by sending these "character-building" and "thought-provoking" chain emails to their younger family members, via family email distribution lists.

One of those old chestnuts carried a heavy-handed lesson, cautioning us against forcing growth on others. It's a fabled story of a young person and their grandparent, spying a wiggling cocoon on a tree branch. The young person wants to help the butterfly inside the cocoon to emerge by forcing the cocoon open. The grandparent has to educate this young one by explaining that "helping" the butterfly this way would actually kill it. That if they opened the cocoon now, they would find a pile of goo. Because it is through the struggle of development that the worm is able to finish its metamorphosis and emerge as its beautiful finished self.

One day, in the audience at a rather large conference, a speaker retold this story as though they were the actual person having a walk the other day with their grandchild. Needless to say, enough people in the audience knew the story and word spread quickly that this speaker was not to be trusted.

Do not try to pass generalized lessons-as-stories off as your own. Someone in the room will know these recycled fables, and needless to say it will do nothing good for your reputation.

Writing Your Talk, Creatively Speaking

By this point, I haven't asked you to actually write anything yet. But those of you who are excellent at thinking on your feet have done the most preparation you've ever done for a talk by reading about how to write a talk. You feel ready to walk on stage, grab a mic, and rock the whole house. I'm envious of your ability and confidence! And if you have the time, I suggest you try the rest of the process (aka writing your talk) just to see if you learn anything from it. You might learn a new tool or perspective, or something new about your own creativity.

After reading about various elements of a talk, you might have some ideas about which ones you could include in your talk. Maybe filling in the template with brief phrases will capture your ideas and intention on one page. Great!

You could also approach writing your Tiny Talk like you'd write a paper: write complete sentences, exactly as you imagine the words emerging from your mouth. This means you will possibly write a lot of words. Maybe 750-1,500 of them, or more if you're really talkative and wordy. If you go this route, you might need to visually reference the template but write out your talk on paper or type it into your computer, so that you have all the room you need. It's easier for most of us to write more than we will need, prioritizing everything we could say into what we absolutely must say, and then making selective cuts.

Overall, I encourage you to let your creativity run in the pure generation of words. Just write! When you feel a surge of energy, don't pay attention to word count — just write it all down as it pops into your head.

I find this difficult, as I am used to editing my own work and will sometimes edit as I write. Editing as you write is not great for energy, and neither is expecting a perfect talk on your first draft. So try to let go of your need for your first draft to emerge on the page in front of you as a perfect final product. Accept that your first draft will be messy and imperfect. Embrace it. There are steps later to edit and practice, so that you can refine your talk into something you are happy with and proud of.

Humans are naturally curious. We're born that way and sometimes life tries to pry it out of us, in service of output, results, efficiency, or productivity. Public speaking rewards the curious. As you create your talk, you may start to question what you actually know, which will lead you to Google searches, blog posts, TikToks, perhaps a short trip to the library. Don't let me dissuade you, but do be practical and let your time constraints guide you. In other words, cultivate your curiosity in general, but only cultivate it for this talk as you realistically have time. At some point, you have to get writing.

So get writing!

4
PRACTICE YOUR TINY TALK

Excuses for Skipping Practice

I bet half of you will dismiss me as soon as I suggest, "You need to practice your talk." So allow me to address the most common reasons people try to rationalize not practicing their talk.

"I'm just going to read my talk anyway. No need to practice! The words are there."

Cool. That's a personal choice and I support that. And you may still find with a practice run or two that there are phrases and word choices that look great on paper / screen, but sound different from how it played in your head, or even are just difficult to enunciate. You might end up stumbling around alliteration in front of the real audience, when a practice run could have isolated that area and allowed you to make more confident and informed choices.

Also, most people who read their speeches have practiced them. They know when they will pause, when they will look up and make eye contact with someone in the audience, when they will get softer in volume, and when they will read a cluster of words in rapid succession. They know when they will look back at their notes, and where they left off. They do not lose their place. They do these things because they have practiced. Even if you plan to read, please make sure you practice reading.

"I don't need to. I'm really good on my feet."

You probably are. But this talk does not represent you thinking on your feet. You decided earlier that this talk was important enough for you to do the work of creating differently than you've created before. Honor the work you've done, honor yourself, and honor the audience by moving with conviction into the practice phase.

*Note: There is a tiny percentage of people who can move from writing and editing into speaking in front of a live audience — and do it well. They may be geniuses at "practicing in their heads." If this is you, and you skip practicing 100% of the time, and 100% of the time it comes out as good as it was on paper, then I guess I'm not talking to you. I am talking to everyone else who's trying to get out of practicing.

"I don't want to sound scripted."

The vast majority of the time, the point of practicing is not to memorize your talk, word for word. The first time we practice, we test whether what we've written reflects how we actually speak. This gives us a chance to shape the talk more closely to our natural spoken language patterns. The second time we practice, it's to figure out where the talk flows well, and where it doesn't, giving us a chance to isolate and address problem points. The third time we practice, we can start to internalize the structure of the talk, which is important for us in the event that we wander a little and lose our place. Having internalized the structure means we have a mental map of where we should be, and how to make our way back to the path if we get off track.

On the flip side, even if your talk is very short, your memory is very good, and you accidentally memorize your script word for word, you can still deliver it in a spontaneous style (good actors do this all the time), or you can decide on the fly to "riff" on your talk in certain spots — to allow yourself chances to speak spontaneously. You'll of course want to be sure you have time to take these liberties.

You've spent more time reading through these arguments and counter arguments than you would spend on a practice session. So let's practice!

Practice on Your Own

You've managed to get your fingers off the keyboard to stop your endless editing, you've taken a break, and now you are ready to move into the next phase: practice.

I strongly suggest that you practice on your own first. These are your words, and they represent your talk and the experience you want to create with it. Before you let others influence your work, give it a run on your own. Experience how the talk sounds and feels to you.

Set aside 30 minutes or so, turn off music and any other distractions, and dive in.

Spoiler alert: It won't be perfect the first time you run through it.

Most people will experience some or all of these during their first practice run:

1. A sentence or phrase looked great on paper but sounded unnatural, stilted, or forced when said out loud.

2. Your talk moved from one section to the next with no obvious connection, and you started to feel like you made wild leaps of logic, requiring your audience to follow along in faith behind you.

3. The metaphorical plane is up in the air and you are not clear how to land it. Or, you wrote a closing so abrupt that you parachuted to the ground and left your audience on the plane, in the sky, without you (I call this the "parachute close," when you're done talking and would rather parachute out than figure out how to land the plane for the benefit of your audience).

4. The talk is not smooth. It's quite bumpy and occasionally jarring and it starts to chip away at your confidence before you've even finished the first practice run.

Please be assured that ALL OF THESE ARE COMPLETELY NORMAL, perhaps multiple times in the same talk. You *want* all these things to happen when you are still in a position to make changes, before you get in front of your live audience. The whole point is to identify where things can be improved, now, when there's literally nothing on the line.

So keep pushing through to the end of your first practice run. Don't let yourself back into the safe cave of editing mode, where you can keep tinkering endlessly on screen or paper, and escape the discomfort of hearing your own voice commanding a room.

Only after you've made it to the end of your first practice run should you go back and make a few of the most obvious changes that need making. Then practice out loud those edited sections again.

- If something looked great but sounded weird, work it out now. Rewrite that section to reflect both the meaning you intended, as well as the words you actually say.
- During bumpy parts, consider switching elements of your presentation around for easier flow.
- If the order seems good and you still feel bumps, write some transition statements to connect one section of your talk to the next.
- If you realized after practicing that you didn't have a solid ending, write a short ending now. An easy closing is to restate or repeat your message one last time, wish your audience well, and say, "Thank you.".

If you want, you can go through the process alone a couple more times: isolate trouble spots → improve them → practice those edited spots. Then run through the whole talk again, start to finish.

Here is some advice from this historically chronic over-tinkerer and recovering under-practicer:

1. Even at this stage, do not aim for "perfection," whatever that means. If you can feel 70-80% satisfied, i.e.

you think you have a solid, basic talk, you will be in great shape for a practice audience.

2. The goal is that each time you go back to edit and practice a rewritten section or two, you emerge from it feeling more certain about your talk as a whole. If you are feeling less certain, you may need a break to clear your mind. Take a walk, listen to music, vacuum your home. Come back after you've enjoyed some distance and time.

Practice for Performance

If your talk isn't for a while yet, you certainly have the luxury of practicing a few times for performance. After the structure is set and you feel confident with the words, you can focus entirely on performance.

When I use the term "performance" here, know that I'm not suggesting you put on a mask (literal or metaphorical) and become someone else. I am talking about focusing on ways you deliver your talk.

Consider "performance elements" of a typical talk:

Body language

- **Posture.** Openness of your body will convey openness to the audience. Keep your shoulders back and your head high. Look in the mirror — many of us slouch as our normal standing posture.

- **Gestures.** What kinds of gestures can you make with your hands that will help to communicate parts of your talk that could use extra energy, visual focus, or amplification? On the flip side, be sure you aren't overdoing the same gestures, which can get uncomfortable and taxing for an audience to watch.
- **The things you might be holding in your hand,** such as a mic, notes, reading glasses, etc. It's a good idea to check in with your event coordinator to confirm whether you'll have a mic and if so, if it will be handheld. This alone may help you decide whether or not to use notes, and if you do, what kind of notes will be best.
- **Glasses.** Some speakers will wear glasses when reading from or referencing their notes, and then they will take them off to address the audience directly. They'll bounce back and forth from one mode to the other. If you do this, be sure you practice with your glasses this way, and that you have a hand free to manage them.

Movement on stage

If you have an actual stage, elevated from the audience, you will have stairs to ascend and descend. Thinking ahead to the shoes you'll be wearing, the process of navigating stairs, etc. may help. Maybe you can have a practice run of your talk at the venue, with the shoes and clothes you're wearing for the talk. A true dress rehearsal.

Even if you won't be standing on a formal stage, you will certainly have an area of the room that Is visually different from the rest of the room and will be treated as the stage. If you know that you will have lots of room to move around, consider whether movement will enhance or detract from your presentation.

Facial expressions

Your facial expressions can communicate a lot to your audience, in addition to your words, and sometimes without any words at all. Much will depend on how close you are to the audience and how well they can see your face.

But don't underestimate the power of facial expressions to guide your own feelings. Even if your audience can't see your facial expressions clearly, you will probably feel as your face emotes. As the saying goes, motion causes emotion.

Tone of voice

When we present, our voice is an endlessly versatile instrument. We can apply the same techniques musicians use for endless expression.

- **Range.** Think of your vocal range as the area your voice covers from its highest pitch (as some of us talk to babies or animals) to its lowest pitch (a la James Earl Jones' Darth Vader). The average person's vocal range for speaking isn't very wide. When we are on stage, giving a talk, we can expand that range a bit and it can heighten emotion without coming across as melodramatic. Or maybe melodrama is what you want.
- **Dynamics.** Similarly, your normal dynamic range (at least for your "inside voice") probably doesn't vary much in everyday conversation. In a talk, experiment with expanding your louds and softs just a bit. Say,

5-10%. This can be used to great effect without seeming unnatural.

- **Tempo.** When we are relaxed, we usually settle into a comfortable-to-us tempo that balances the pace of our brain producing words with our mouths actually speaking them. On stage, when you've already given the words a lot of thought and you may have a bit of adrenaline coursing through you, it wouldn't be surprising if you sped up the tempo of your spoken voice a fair bit. If that's the energy you want to bring, go for it. However, if the event is more solemn or laid back, be sure to practice your talk at a tempo more suitable for the occasion.

- **Pauses.** There's a lot of power in silence. Don't be afraid of it, if it happens when you don't plan it. Pauses give the audience time for a message to sink in. Pauses add welcome contrast to word density. Pauses, when employed with conviction by a speaker, communicate a sense of confidence that is contagious.

- **Texture, color, and dimension.** The quality of your voice is different throughout the day. When you first wake up, your voice is probably gravelly, as your body normalizes to "all systems online" mode. Not having spoken all night, your throat is dry and your vocal cords are out of practice. It may take a bit for your voice to warm up. After you've had your morning beverage and made the morning greeting rounds, you're probably warmed up and your voice sounds correspondingly warm and smooth. If you go to a sports game and participate actively from the stands, you will find that your voice sounds faint and strained.

While these versions of your voice are not being actively called on, you *can* explore different textures, color, and dimension in your voice.

If you've ever done impressions of other people, you know what this means. When I sing an early-2000 Britney Spears song, I know to constrict the air flow in my throat and sing through my nose as much as possible. When I (try to) sing Mariah Carey, I am searching for a quality of clarity, like a bell, and I know I will get to the top of my range and still only reach one full octave below her whistle tones (IYKYK). When I (try to) sing Whitney Houston, I'm only ever singing at full volume and power with all the air at the base of my diaphragm. All three of these singers have wildly different textures, colors, and dimensions to their voices and while I'll never give a talk in one of their voices, I can definitely use the techniques I've learned from mimicking their voices to explore texture, color, and dimension in my own voice.

For a tiny book, this list of ideas to push the performance value of your talk is plenty. Go wild and have fun practicing!

Practice the Pauses—and Silence Too

It's common for us to "talk to ourselves" out loud while practicing those first couple of times. The thing is, the part of your brain that is hearing you talk isn't differentiating between your presentation and your self-talk. So it might be remembering self-talk instead of real talk, or getting overwhelmed by all the words and not committing much to useful memory at all.

Think about presentations you've watched where the speaker has lost their place and talked to themselves, in front of you. If they happened to say something funny, maybe it diffused tension in the room. More often than not, they probably said things that they didn't intend to, and maybe what they said ended up detracting from their message. Maybe what they said in that live self-talk made you start to feel nervous *for them*. Not great.

So when you practice your talk on your own, be sure to practice the silence that happens when you need to turn to the next page, or take a look at the clock. A funny thing happens with time in these moments, where in reality (and to your audience) only a second of silence has occurred, but to us on the stage, time has suddenly become elastic and that same second *feels* like an eternity.

Purposeful silence in your talk can function as pauses do, for you as well as for your audience. Your job is not to fill every second with words; your job is to deliver a message with impact. An ongoing stream of words will rob your audience of opportunities to internalize your message, mainly because every word will seem to be equal. You may win the battle of words, but you will risk losing the war of meaning.

Here are some places in your talk where pausing makes a lot of sense:

1. Pause for laughter after humorous moments. Take note of the delay for the joke to hit.

2. Pause strategically after a thought-provoking question. Look up to see if the wheels are turning in the heads of your practice audience people.

3. Pause to find your place in your notes and ground yourself again. These occasional pauses allow the audience to process what they're hearing, and for the most meaningful ideas to find a place in their longer-term memory.

Practice with a Timer

At this point, you feel solid about your message, the structure, and the flow. Let's see how close you are to the time allotted.

Don't get too technical with this one. If you record a practice run, your video will be time stamped and you won't need to "time" your talk separately.

It shouldn't surprise you that even in a short-form presentation, there are areas we can predictably get stuck and lose time:

- The opening / introduction. It makes sense that we lose time here, because we are "just getting warmed up." On the flip side, playing loose with our words will likely compromise our timeline. I strongly suggest making this part as concise as possible by design, and delivering the words as close as you can to how they are written.

- Stories. We can run long when we tell stories by adding back in, on the fly, all the details we love to share but actually do nothing to push the narrative forward and give us the momentum we are trying to build. Again, stay disciplined during practice to give just the information and detail that helps you build momentum and drives the talk forward.

- The closing. If we don't have a strong closing planned, we can wander to the finish line. And as we know, a lot of wandering usually results in taking more time than is necessary.

Keep these three sections as simple and tight as possible, even in practice.

How much time do you really have? Will someone have a timer and play music to cue you offstage if you go over time? Alternatively, do you want to be the speaker with a 15-minute talk, holding everyone up from eating hot food, after every other speaker only needed 5 minutes? There's a lot here I don't know, but that you can find out about your situation. So get clear about expectations and put on your Good Human hat and edit intelligently.

After you've practiced with a timer, you might be surprised that you are finishing up quite quickly. You can decide now: Is this the best presentation I can give in the given time constraints? If it is, for heaven's sake, stop there. Don't feel the need to glop more words into your presentation just because you have time to say more. If you have made your point clearly and compellingly, you are done! Your audience will love you and the presentation will be even more powerful because of your succinctness.

You may be ending quite early because you edited out a big story before you even practiced. (Sometimes we do this — old sophomore high school English habits die hard). If you do think there's more power in adding to your talk, and you know you have time, use your best discretion to add a story, a metaphor, or a joke.

I find that my challenge is often the opposite: after practicing, I am way over time. I need to trim. Any editing process offers the same advice, whether you're a writer, a composer, or a fashion designer: be ready to kill your darlings. As much as you love a specific joke or story, you might need to cut it because it really is a bonus appendage: nice to have if you need it, but simply extra weight if you don't. Cut it.

I hope that you won't get to the point where you have to choose between editing the outline and removing the very details that give your talk dimension, texture, and life. Because at a certain point, you may have to choose, for time. My choice nearly all the time will be to cut structure and preserve the depth.

Practice with an Audience

Most of us will benefit from practicing in front of a live human audience. I've suggested that you practice alone first and edit, and do that a few more times before going in front of a human audience because people can be wildly unpredictable in their feedback. I want you to develop a sense of confidence about your talk before you put yourself in a situation where someone may unintentionally have you second-guessing structure and content before you've even gotten to 75-80% confidence about those elements.

Remember that you can practice in front of a real-time audience via FaceTime or Zoom or some other digital format as well as in real life.

When your practice audience is ready, jump right into it. Don't feel like you need to explain a bunch of things up front, or otherwise give a "speech before the speech."

It's ideal if you are practicing this talk as close to what you imagine in your head when you're in front of your practice audience, even though you may only be practicing with an audience of one.

I have a lot more suggestions in the next section about feedback in general. But after practicing in front of a live audience, you will probably seek and get direct feedback. Remember that hearing it doesn't mean you're obligated to act on it.

After your practice run with a live audience, you might start the feedback by saying something like, "THANK YOU for helping me with my talk. I'm excited to hear what you think, so I'll listen carefully and take time to consider it all. The main feedback I'm looking for is ____. How did I do?" And what you insert in ____ can determine how the rest of your conversation goes. By being specific about ____ you will help them address your most pressing need first. And everything they say after that is a bonus.

For feedback during the practice stage, I'll offer this simple advice:

1. Write it all down, and say thank you after each new fresh piece of feedback. Mean it. Your practice audience is helping and they are giving their feedback with the best of intentions. Try your best not to get defensive or even feel like you have to explain certain choices. Listen, listen, listen. Say thank you again after they've given all their feedback.

2. After they've spoken, categorize / prioritize the feedback into 3 groups: "this confirms what I was thinking and feeling"; "this is about the structure and general message of the talk"; and "this is about the word choice, style, and delivery".

   * Everything that confirmed what you knew: If it requires changes, make the changes.

   * Comments about the structure and general message: you have invested a lot of time and effort into this talk, so whether you take these suggestions should be

based on how well this person's feedback has served you before. If you've taken their prior feedback to make changes and it was well received, then weigh that more heavily than if this person has given feedback that wasn't as useful or productive.

* Feedback about word choice, style, and delivery: You know yourself, your topic, and this event best. The choice of whether to change any of these things based on your practice audience's feedback is entirely yours.

3. Practice the parts you changed / added. If you have time and it will make you feel better, practice it again from start to finish, so you are comfortable with the new flow.

Some feedback will persuade you to make changes, and some suggestions are merely options to consider. Fundamentally, I think it's OK to not take action on all feedback we are given. When I am asked for my advice, I'll often preface with: "Take what's useful, and discard the rest." While your practice audience may not feel as gracious about the feedback they give you, I'll tell you a secret: *You get to choose in the end.* You don't have to tell your practice audience in the moment what you're taking and what you're discarding. Just do what you want to make your talk better.

Practice with Your Tools + Props

Whatever you are going to present with, practice with those things. Don't overthink, and don't get in your head. Be aware, make decisions, and practice.

You might not have all the answers and that is OK. Whatever answers you can get, let them guide how you practice. You're aiming to practice under conditions as close to reality as possible.

1. Microphone

Will you have a microphone? Will you need to hold it in one hand, so your notes will be in your other hand? (And how will you turn pages if you need to) ? Will you be able to use a wearable, clip-on style? If so, will it wrap around your head like a gym trainer, or clip onto your clothes (and how might it change your wardrobe choice to have a big battery pack clipped to your waistband)?

2. Notes

Can you fit them all on one page? If you have two pages of notes, do you prefer for them to be printed front and back on the same sheet, or on two separate sheets?

If your goal is to reference your notes and not read them, be sure you have very few words written on your notes — phrases, really, to prompt you to remember what to say — and practice using them so that you are also practicing to improve your memory.

Will you require separate reading glasses? Be sure to pack them if you'll need them.

3. Slides

The best slides are simple. They should enhance, not distract from, your presentation. So don't use the slides as an excuse to go down some bunny trail and avoid the main intent of practice. If you *must* use slides, ask yourself what the bare minimum information or reinforcement is required to make your communication of the message stronger.

If you will be close to the computer that's running the slide show, practice navigating to your slide deck; opening and launching it; and advancing through it using the keyboard.

If you will use a presentation remote, practice advancing through your slides using the remote.

If people don't need a visual to track with what you're saying, press the button to "mute" the screen (press B on the keyboard or the corresponding button on your presenter remote, if there is one).

Most importantly, have at least three plans for your slides. For instance, Plan A is that you copy your slide show to the laptop that's running all the slides. Plan B is to copy them to a memory stick in case that laptop crashes and they bring you a last-minute replacement. Plan C is to put them on Google Drive so you can download them to the new computer (be sure to know your password. As I mentioned, this is not my first rodeo with presentations).

4. Props

If you plan to use other presentation props and want to display or reveal them, it's time to practice as best you can how those work into your presentation.

Maybe you're toasting a groom and want to share his college sports jersey at a certain point during your talk. It's helpful to plan how you will fold, transport, and "reveal" it at the moment of greatest impact. Keep in mind if you're holding a mic, you'll only have one hand available for this, or you will need to coordinate with an assistant. (Practice with that assistant if you can.)

Maybe you'll be in a conference room with no slides but a flip chart or other display board. Can you pre-write or pre-draw your prop? Or is it more effective to draw during the talk, in which case you may want to bring your own markers (for paper or dry-erase?).

Visualization Can Help

Some of us do well with visualization during our practice. As you're practicing, imagine looking out at the audience and seeing familiar faces, smiling and nodding in affirmation, laughing at your funny moments and leaning in to your talk. You can also visualize from the back of the room, seeing yourself at the front, where you are standing, and how you are carrying yourself with confidence. These are just mental tricks to help us, even during practice, get more "in the zone" and increase our confidence and ease on presentation day.

Why We Practice

There are so many benefits to practicing.

1. We need to hear what we sound like, to ourselves.

2. What we write and what we say can be very different. You the Writer is not always You the Speaker. On paper, words can look brilliant, but said out loud, they could sound and feel flat. Practice is the real start of your editing process.

3. The order of your talk may look logical as an essay, but said aloud, may reveal some unexpected twists, drastic turns, and leaps of logic that are difficult for a listener to follow. You may find that re-ordering elements of your talk, or adding some transition statements, will smooth things out so your audience can follow you successfully from start to finish.

4. Practice helps you build trust in yourself and your words. The first practice run is almost always bumpy, for every single one of us. But if you trust the process first, that practice will lead to better results, you will be able to edit your talk into something that you trust. And eventually you'll extend that trust to your abilities.

5. You'll get clear about where in your talk there's power and magic. You can start internalizing the structure of your talk, and key phrases and ideas will plant themselves as milestones on this journey you're leading for your audience.

6. You can get a real sense of timing. In the last section, we estimated that a 5-minute talk will fit, on average, about 750 words, and a 10-minute talk about 1,500 words. But that rule of thumb will vary on a lot of variables. What's most useful is how long it takes *you*. How fast you talk will affect how many words you can fit in a minute, so after you've practiced your Tiny Talk, you'll have a good idea how well it fits into the time allotted.

And over several talks, you will be able to calculate an average number of words per minute FOR YOU.

In summary: The last thing you want is for your practice run to also be the actual talk itself. So practice!

5
GIVE YOUR TINY TALK

At the Event

Your bag is packed. You arrive at the event. Now what?

I encourage you to enjoy the proceedings.

Sometimes we go into that over-prep or over-practice mode, which overwhelms our brain. Give your brain a chance to file all that good stuff into longer-term memory. Stop thinking about it for a bit.

Once on-site, try not to think about your talk. Don't give yourself a chance to get in your own head. Other people will be there, giving their own speeches and adding to the experience — so be present with them and experience every moment before you go up.

If you find your mind repeatedly wandering back to your talk, turn your attention instead to specific people or groups. Notice their energy, their enthusiasm, the connections happening before your very eyes.

Have a couple of small-talk questions in your head to ask everyone, so it keeps you focused on other people and the event at large. "What do you think so far?" " Are you having a great time?" "What's your favorite thing you've heard today?" Keep it easy, keep it light, and stay present.

All of this will ground you in the spirit of the event and connect you to the others present, even before you've begun your talk. Your role is to contribute to this shared experience, and now you can deliver your talk with the intention you so carefully prepared, as well as the spirit of the events unfolding around you and with you. Become one, together.

Trust Your Audience — and Yourself

It's almost go time! At the very least, you should make a quick list of items you need for this talk, like your notes, a bottle of water, a presentation remote, and any props or visuals that you plan to share.

Depending on how complex the event details and what kind of planner you are, you may also want to note the clothes, shoes, and accessories you'll wear. You may be comforted having thought through small details that can really ease your mind and help you stay in the moment, with your audience, when it's time.

Are you feeling anxious or nervous even though you feel good about the work you've put in? Maybe you're worried about how the audience will react to your talk. The remedy?
Trust your audience. They are there for you.

The default mode of every audience is to offer hope and support. Before you've begun talking, your audience is hopeful that the whole event, including your talk, will be great.

They are ready to support you because they don't want you to have a bad talk. If you give a bad talk, they have to listen to a bad talk, and by default, they don't want that. So take comfort in this: from the start, you are operating from a position of advantage.

The only obvious exception to this is if you're speaking to a hostile audience. A politician hosting a town hall full of angry constituents won't experience the default setting of "hopeful, supportive audience" though I bet at least a couple will be. But if you're a politician preparing for a town hall, you're probably not reading this book right now. And if you are a politician preparing for an angry mob, it's possible that nothing you say will help. In those cases, listening is often a far better approach, and you should be unsurprised that I also facilitate a workshop on that.

Perhaps you are pitching an idea from a position that isn't popular or well known. You may choose to strike a persuasive tone from the start of your talk. Acknowledge your audience's hesitation up front, perhaps sharing a point of view they didn't have before that talk. You will depend on the data, stories, and testimonials you share to do the job — so choose wisely. Remember my disclaimer at the start of this book that the Tiny Talk Model assumes a friendly or neutral audience.

I want to be sure that you take a moment to acknowledge the work you've done so far. If you've read from the beginning to now, and put the book down to actually write a talk, you've invested a couple of hours on your talk already. Great job! You're almost there.

Trust in the thinking, preparation, and practice you've put in so far. Trust the work. Trust yourself. Trust your audience. It's going to go great.

But first...

A Note About Notes

During my first keynote speech, I held court on stage for AN HOUR in front of two hundred people. As a workshop facilitator and Tiny Talk expert, this long form presentation was a new and terrifying experience. I planned for this keynote from the day I said yes to the moment I walked on stage, including hours of writing and practice, and several coaching sessions to help me prepare and practice.

I knew I didn't want to use notes, but an hour is a long time to deliver a presentation from memory. I had slimmed my notes from the full talk over many pages to just the headers and main stories to a series of emojis. I printed these emojis on sticker paper and glued them to my presenter remote. It didn't matter that the print was so small I couldn't clearly decipher the emojis — the "notes" provided me with the emotional comfort I needed.

Now, you get to decide for yourself whether you want to use notes during your talk.

Notes vs No Notes

As a presenter I am usually ok using notes. Even when evaluating other speakers, I don't have an automatic aversion to their using notes. I'd argue that most audiences are ok with their speaker using notes, if they aren't being used in a distracting way.

Depending on context and expectations, some audiences will prefer less reliance on notes (a work presentation where you are conveying confidence and exercising persuasion to secure budget for a new idea) while others are perfectly acceptable environments to rely on notes (a 50th birthday toast). So consider the context and expectations.

Many audiences are just fine with any presenter using notes, as long as they aren't reading from them. Occasionally glancing at them to make sure you're on track is not the same as nervously reading your talk, word for word, from a sheaf of papers rattling in your shaking hands.

If you decide to use notes, how will you use them? Specifically, do you plan to read your talk word-for-word, or will you read short sections and then ad-lib in between? Or will you mainly speak conversationally and only glance at your notes to make sure you are tracking correctly?

Reading vs. Referencing

If your goal is to give your talk while keeping eye contact with your audience most of the time, you want to get clear on the difference between reading and referencing your notes. Reading your notes often means that every word you plan to say is in front of you at the time you are giving your talk. Referencing your notes means that you're glancing at your notes every 30 or 60 seconds to get your bearings or check that you're on track — you should need very few notes for this. If you intend to only reference your notes during your talk, but you walk in with pages of notes containing complete sentences, you will end up reading them. Do yourself a favor and slim down your notes if you intend to only reference them.

If you plan to read your talk, record yourself and watch it on playback. You want to be sure that you are looking up from your notes often enough to make eye contact occasionally, before you go back to reading. (Emma Thompson does this so, so well. One might argue that she actually has her whole talk memorized, and the paper is just a prop for her excellent acting.)

If your goal is to rely on your notes very little, make sure you practice using slimmed-down notes. It does no good to keep practicing with notes that contain full sentences and paragraphs, and then go in front of your live audience with a graphic doodled on a sticky note. Practice using the notes you will use in real life. Sometimes this is an iterative process: Your first practice run is with full printed sentences. Your notes for your third practice run may contain just the topics of each of the three sections of your talk. And who knows? The final practice run could be done from referencing just one drawing.

Printed vs. Electronic Notes

There's obviously a risk in using paper for your notes. There's always a chance you could lose your notes. You may be at a destination wedding and your hotel can't print your talk for you. You could be of a certain age, and the glasses you wore during practice are not the glasses you have in front of you during your talk, rendering the words on the page unreadable to you.

This is not to say that electronic notes are inherently better. You can delete files by accident. Phone screens are smaller than standard printer paper, for those of us juggling multiple pairs of glasses. I've also found that when speakers use their phones for their notes, more members of their audience will seem to mirror the act of looking at their phone. I'm not sure if it's subconscious mirroring or if the audience feels less connected to the speaker when the speaker is looking at their phone.

There's no absolute right or wrong answer for every situation. As in nearly everything else in life, context matters. So consider the context for your talk, expectations of others (your boss?), the venue, and other resources. And be prepared with a Plan A, a Plan B, and a Plan C. In the past, my Plan A has been paper, Plan B is my iPad, and Plan C is my phone.

Also remember that no notes is a great Plan A.

And now...

Open your notes, accept the microphone, take a deep breath, smile, and begin!

Notice all the people making eye contact with you. Meet their eyes and send the phrase you're saying specifically to them.

When your humor gets a laugh – pause. Smile and relax your shoulders, take a cleansing breath, and give that laughter a few seconds to subside. Find your place in your notes. Pick up where you left off.

When you make a point and it lands, watch the group. Listen to the collective breath you just took away. Take a beat and soak it in. Be with your audience, a community of people, present and responsive and LIVING IN THE MOMENT.

You are doing this!

6
RECEIVE FEEDBACK ON YOUR TINY TALK

Be Careful Reading Your Own Press

If you're even halfway good at giving talks — and I think you will be — you will help people. You'll hear some flattering things. They will be true, and you should celebrate these moments of connection.

I also suggest that you keep this feedback balanced with the feedback you receive that shines light on areas of opportunity for growth, your own feedback from you to you, and the reason you gave the talk.

The talks will benefit you, yes. But they are also for others.

Balance. That's the point.

Remember that many people are used to only offering positive feedback. Because of our cultural conditioning, expect far more positive feedback on your talk than "constructive" feedback.

Depending on who you ask, some will tell you that critical feedback means you "are not for this person." They are not your audience and you should not concern yourself with the small mindedness of others.

Others will advise you to take every bit of feedback to heart. Which is well-intentioned, but misses the reality that not all feedback is good feedback. Taking everything people think about us to heart can lead to personal anxiety anytime we feel feedback heading our way. Not to mention, eventually we will get two pieces of conflicting feedback about the same thing, resulting in confusion, paralysis, and an increasing numbness to the very thing that has the most potential outside of ourselves to help us grow.

And others will say that you should never pay attention to the most positive and most negative feedback; ignore the outliers and only focus on the feedback in the middle.

These ways of processing feedback present severe challenges and limits when we abide by them as hard and fast rules. We will benefit the most from feedback when we give every bit of it a true, fair shake — and then do what is immediately actionable and desirable, and either banking (for later consideration) or discarding (it truly is not useful feedback) the rest. Sorting through feedback this way requires self-assurance, time, and emotional maturity that many of us don't readily have.

After your talk, you will probably get feedback. And while I facilitate a half-day workshop on feedback, where we go into the why as well as the how, I'm going to "bottom-line" a process for you to be able to take the feedback you get from your Tiny Talk and use what you can to improve your next talk.

We Want Feedback

The vast majority of the feedback you get will be positive and supportive. It will be clear how much you cared and how much you prepared, and every audience appreciates that you thought better of them than to waste their time, or risk a good moment by winging it.

We all have developed different ways of receiving feedback, and I'll bet most of these ways happened by accident. If you were like me, and got some harsh feedback early in your life, you may reflexively brace and arm yourself every time you feel feedback coming. You may be shielding yourself from negative comments, but may find that the positive feedback isn't reaching you, either.

I've heard that an entire generation after mine grew up with ONLY positive feedback. How nice for you, haha. But that could mean your perception of yourself in the world is vastly different from how others see you. Misalignment of this kind makes it difficult to advance through life with much certainty, or with friends.

Public speakers need feedback from others to do our job better. After all, we speak to connect. And when we don't connect well with someone, or at all, it helps to understand why.

Before I share with you a really useful process for receiving feedback, I want to share an idea about feedback that you may not have heard before: Receiving feedback from someone does not obligate you to change.

When it comes to feedback, imagine yourself on a field of play. We will give the person who is giving you feedback the benefit of the doubt, and assume they are on your team.

They want to share feedback to help you improve, possibly even to help the team do better. The person who's giving you feedback is in possession of the ball, and they are about to pass you the ball. As the intended receiver, your job is to complete the pass. That's it.

The next best play may be to pass the ball to another teammate. You don't have to run one specific play once you have the ball. You don't even need to keep the ball in play. In fact, you may realize that the ball is from the game one court over and doesn't even belong on your court. When someone gives you feedback, you aren't responsible for how they give it to you. Your only job is to successfully receive the pass.

Start to separate receiving the feedback from deciding what to do with the feedback. These are not only two different things; they can happen at two different times.

How to Receive Feedback on Your Tiny Talk

At large and busy events, most people will approach you after a talk with a simple word of thanks or encouragement, and it's appropriate for you to simply accept it with a smile and two words: "Thank you."

I do NOT recommend that you refuse the feedback, or deflect it. "Oh, it was no big deal." "I just kind of threw this speech together last night." "It was nothing compared to the closing speaker — she was stellar!" This makes the feedback giver feel like they have to reassure you now, and are responsible for your weirdness. Don't be weird. Say thank you and keep it moving.

I've come to appreciate the unpredictability of the post-talk conversation. Sometimes people want to gush. Sometimes there is a specific idea or phrase that resonated with them, and they have a story of their own to share. Accept this connection. You did your part and now they want to reciprocate.

And occasionally — this is more likely to happen at work than in a social setting — someone will want to give you notes on your talk. Something didn't land right with them, or flew in the face of what they believed. Maybe you told a story that missed the mark for them, or you hold a conviction that they simply do not share, and they must clear their conscience before they clear out of the room.

Here is how I handle that feedback:

1. Be present for it.

Focus on the feedback giver, which may be hard given how busy the environment is, and how long the line is of people who want to talk with you. Stay loose and limber. Anything could be coming at you. Clear your mind of expectation. This could be a curve ball. It could be the fastest, most direct pitch ever headed your way.

2. Explore the feedback, if you are genuinely curious to hear more.

Ask questions, keeping your questions open and your tone light.

3. Advocate for yourself and your talk, if the feedback giver indicates they want to hear from you.

Advocating does not mean defending your talk, or rationalizing the choices you made. If the feedback giver has suggested that data you shared was not as complete as what they would have liked, it may be helpful to you both to quickly explain your process. Simply add your additional perspective, if you believe it's truly helpful. But this step, directly following a talk, is optional for both you and the feedback giver.

4. Resolve the feedback conversation with a simple "thank you."

We live in a confrontation-averse culture. We are uncomfortable being candid with people when it comes to offering performance feedback that identifies opportunities for growth. I personally know people who will not offer anything remotely resembling "constructive criticism," opting instead to be a one-person cheer squad, even if they must remain silent when there is nothing to celebrate. This is both cowardly and unhelpful, and contributes to stagnation and slow decline, as we are unable to address the very things we need to change to improve our situation. Over time, this conditions us to expect only positive, loving, supportive feedback, when what we need is the hard-to-hear feedback that will help us move from ok to exceptional.

Unfortunately, of the small percentage of people who are comfortable giving feedback, many take the phrase "brutal feedback" literally, and have neither tact nor grace nor balance when they so willingly "let you have it." This approach to giving feedback can condition us over time to wince when someone says they have feedback for us. We dash into our office to put on a full suit of armor for the impact.

The best news is that we don't need people to be skilled at giving feedback. We only need to work on our ability to receive all feedback, process it, and change based on the highest-quality feedback we receive.

Feedback from You to You

Your most important audience might be you. You have to live with yourself, after all. You've heard from everyone else. Now share some feedback with yourself. Unless they were in your practice audience, no one in the real audience knew your plan. But you know how well things went according to plan.

I'll bet that something you forgot to say that you thought diminished your talk made no difference to your audience. You might have added a story or gone a little over time, but were glad to have added that extra sparkle about the guest of honor anyway.

Open a note on your phone, and capture your thoughts as soon as you get a private moment. Record a voice memo if you prefer. By the next day, you may forget many of the fine points of the experience.

A basic debrief includes three simple questions:
1. What went well?
2. What should I change next time?
3. What did I learn from this experience?

Given the Tiny Talk Model, two additional questions from you to you are:

4. Did the audience feel the way I hoped they would feel from my talk?
5. Did I communicate my message well? Did it land with the audience?

If you want to — and you know you won't obsess about it — give yourself a quick rating of the talk on a 1-10 scale, with 10 being a dream come true.

Something that helped me gain perspective early-on was also to objectively rate what others thought of my talk, based on their feedback. I was always a far harsher critic than anyone, often by magnitudes. This comparison (how you felt it went vs. how the feedback suggests the audience felt it went) can calibrate your sense of your speaking effectiveness over time.

Do It Again

I was a music kid. Band, choir, orchestra — I was in them all. By the time I graduated college, I'd performed with probably a hundred ensembles, developed a fantastic repertoire, and played memorable solos under the batons of diverse conductors. I'd even tried on different pre-performance green room personalities, from laid-back background singer to high-strung, bouquet-accepting diva.

But the first time I was asked to give a presentation at work, just a few years later, I was stumped. I would not have an instrument to hide behind, or the work of a centuries-dead composer to interpret. It would be me at the front of the room, saying my words. No need to interpret, perform, or do anything other than share my thoughts with a willing audience.

I was terrified.

But I did the work. I went to the library, and the bookstore, and I read everything I could about public speaking. I learned a lot of ideas and techniques, but the thing that helped me improve the most was just doing it. Accepting that presenting parts of my work was the best way to prove my worth — and I started getting better than average at it.

A couple of jobs and many Tiny Talks later, I stood in front of a room of executive leaders, seeking support for a program my team was developing. After my talk, one of those leaders approached me. I was ready, of course, to answer questions about the program. She, however, had an entirely different topic in mind.

"Have you ever thought about training?" She asked me.

"Training?" I asked in clarification. Like, at a gym? How did we get here conversationally?

"Training. Public speaking. Professionally."

"No, is that something people do?"

"It's something that a lot of people do. I do it in my role as a Regional Director, but I also do it outside of that job. I teach licensing classes in my state and have trained others in the past as my only job. I think you could be really good at it."

She handed me a copy of *Training* magazine. "I was reading this on the plane. Take a look at it sometime."

I didn't forget about this conversation, but I did go back to my regular work, which took me down another path, and then another. But she planted a seed in my head, and some six or seven years later I was running a business doing exactly what Ms. Kay Evans had suggested on that fateful day. I wasn't consciously following steps to build a public speaking business, but the seed Kay had planted in my mind was nurtured and cultivated. Several years later, I was facilitating and public speaking full time, and eventually also teaching and coaching others to do it.

Kay's advice was a seed, but in retrospect that conversation included a lot of strong feedback. She was telling me that, while I was projecting Program Manager vibes, she was reading a strong undercurrent of public speaker – so strong and so promising that she could see a future for me that I didn't know existed.

My job in that moment wasn't to tell her she was right or wrong. My job was to complete the pass that she was throwing. Message received.

I didn't consciously act on her feedback, but every time I was offered another opportunity to speak, I took it. And the feedback on that talk or workshop would be so strong that I'd earn another opportunity, and then another. Over time, I was able to use feedback to build a career and a business that I loved.

You don't have to build a speaking business after giving a few Tiny Talks. But you can build anything you want, if you figure out how to take all the feedback you get from other people – whether it's spot-on or way off the mark, graceful or uncomfortably awkward, well intentioned or delivered with a sneer – and make it work for you.

7
DESIGN YOUR LIFE, ONE TINY TALK AT A TIME

You Did It!

You prepared, you practiced, you did the work, you gave your talk. Congrats!

You probably still feel the adrenaline, and because you connected with people, they will keep the good vibes and high energy flowing.

Stay in this moment. Stay with these people, with whom your message resonates. Stay present. Ride the wave.

Once you feel signals in your brain and body unscrambling and relaxing, you can turn your attention to making sense of the experience and the feedback. And after the information processing has been done and you drift off to sleep that night, hopefully you will decide to do it all again.

Your brain thought about the topic, the angles of entry, and the ideas you wanted to communicate.

Your heart imagined the feelings your talk would evoke, the connections you wanted to make in the room, with your audience and among your audience, and maybe even connections you hoped your audience would make with others long after your talk was over.

Your hands went to work writing the words, practicing the gestures, taking the risks to ego.

You did this. You made this!

The Tiny Talk Model is Just One Model

There are so many ways to relate with people, and to connect with them. The Tiny Talk model is just one of them. It's pretty structured, and over time if you keep using it, you may find that it has its best application for you in certain situations, whereas you prefer other presentation models for other situations.

I use the metaphor often that each of us moves through our days with a toolbox. Some of us have a literal toolbox, and all of us have a mental toolbox.

The thing about tools is that we can have the best and highest quality tools in the world, but if we aren't familiar with them and can't use them well, we may as well not have them at all. Practicing to use the tools we have helps us to know how we can make the best use of them. So keep practicing Tiny Talks until you are comfortable knowing when they're the best choice, and how to use them.

If you use the Tiny Talk model often enough, you will internalize it. And eventually you'll find that you can organize short-form presentations in your head, assembling pieces and fitting them in place as they occur to you.

Also over time, you may develop in parallel a confidence in yourself and your ability to "wing it" better. And when you're put on the spot and handed a microphone at a luncheon to introduce the guest speaker, you'll have the tools AND the confidence to pull it off with style and grace. And *that* excites me more than you know.

It's that trust you build in yourself, that thing of substance, that will help you feel ready for each successive opportunity that comes your way — and maybe that trust will embolden you to seek — or better, make — the opportunities you want.

The Tiny Talk Model is a Tool in Your Leadership Toolbox

The specific job of leadership requires tools, too, and the Tiny Talk model is another tool in your toolbox.

Because being a better public speaker, at least in the U.S., automatically carries cachet and implies stronger leadership. And opportunities are offered to those who engender trust from others. If you show others that you trust yourself, it's a lot easier for someone else to offer you that first deposit of trust. And then you get to prove whether you have the goods to back up the show.

People have used their public speaking skills for personal gain for time immemorial. If you do, too, there's no shame in that. But as you grow in your career, in your business, and in your community, I hope you will remember that fundamentally, you're in a position of leadership because people trust you. While it might be easy for you to use words to deceive people, my hope is that you will remember that your voice can do much more than make money.

Some would argue that making money is the easy part.

Making positive change in the world is much harder. Making positive and responsible change in the world is the real work.

When you get close to having enough for yourself and your family, focus more of your time and skill on the communities around you. Speak up for what is right, and help people speak up for themselves, too. When everyone can access a microphone, lots of people can talk at the same time with very few people listening. The competitive advantage lies in your ability to appeal to your audience. So get sharper and help those around you get sharper, too.

The gift of speech, the power of words, the democratization of platform — we have a lot of potential influence at our disposal. And we are often careless about how we use it. Or we don't use it at all.

You can use the tools and skills from your Tiny Talk to make a series of Tiny Talks that are the building blocks of a social media campaign for your side hustle. You can create an online course with each lesson as a Tiny Talk, and start a new passive income stream. You can help a community in recovery by packaging each step of that recovery as a Tiny Talk.

As you build this skill, you will build one of your leadership muscles. If you aren't already, you'll become the go-to person for answers and advice for those closest to you — even when you have neither answers nor advice to give. And I hope that you will do the work inside, to be worthy of leading others in the way they trust you. I also hope you will do the work to build other leadership muscles, so that you are well-rounded in your style.

I haven't even met you yet, and I'm excited about where you can take this.

Let's Change the World with Our Talks

I believe Tiny Talks can change the world.

Tiny Talks inspire curiosity about the world. They require intellectual rigor and commitment to creativity. They demand personal integrity and authenticity. They demonstrate a desire to connect with people.

I've watched people change their own worlds, one Tiny Talk at a time.

I've watched our whole world change in the last 20 years. Some change is substantial, built on a foundation of integrity, where the inspiring and motivating words we hear match the passionate action and hard work behind the scenes.

Other change is composed of words that sound promising, but a look behind the curtain reveals no core and very little substance. Occasionally these folks talk such a big game and do not deliver that they end up in jail, or they should be in jail but somehow avoid it.

It's my hope that more people who have always had the substance but haven't always felt confident about the words will gain a new tool in their leadership tool box with Tiny Talks. The world needs more leaders to step up and enact the change that comes from a smart brain, a good heart, and good, old-fashioned action.

Turn on the news and watch people speak.

Then stop watching and just listen. Listen to the language. Listen for the message.

Modern culture has become a space where any words can be put in community spaces, with no accountability for what's said and who's affected by it. Political debates and town halls are, unfortunately, notorious for people filling space and time with any nonsense language they want.

In a world full of foolishness, let's commit to doing better. Let your truth shine a bright light. Cut through the clutter and the noise. Make it make sense for the rest of us.

We all deserve better. Our kids deserve better. When we consider the legacy we are leaving, think bigger. Let's think beyond trust funds and real estate and ask ourselves what ideas, what community, and what beauty we are building for and leaving to the next generation.

The Future is Yours

Delivering one Tiny Talk will build your confidence, at least a little bit. And that's something to celebrate. In the long arc of your public speaking and leadership, preparing and delivering one Tiny Talk is the equivalent of doing one set of reps one time. I genuinely hope that you keep doing the reps, building your muscle and form and confidence, and ultimately trusting yourself more.

Look around you. Lots of people don't overcome anxiety to develop trust in themselves. They seek constant validation and reassurance from those around them. Sometimes those who seem to be self-confident are actually masking deep insecurity by reflexively and thoughtlessly insisting they're right about things they're quite wrong about. And yet others who trust deeply in themselves manage to live entirely out of touch with reality.

Building real trust in yourself, and calibrating your judgement about how you experience the world in relation to the world itself, is something we get to practice and develop every time we take the risk and do the work of each Tiny Talk.

Over time, our trust in ourselves will grow, and we will feel ready for longer talks, tougher audiences, and more challenging topics.

One talk at a time, you can literally speak your future self into existence. You can make the future into whatever you want it to be. Just don't forget to do the work behind the words, too, and you will be in great shape.

Let's grow!

8
TOOLS + RESOURCES

Scan this QR code for PDF versions of these forms, as well as sample Tiny Talks.

Mental Organization Worksheet

YOU
Who are you?
How are you related / relevant?

_____

_____

_____

_____

MESSAGE
What do you have to say?

_____

_____

_____

_____

_____

AUDIENCE
How do you want them to feel?
What do you want them to do?

_____

_____

_____

_____

Tiny Talk Template
5 minutes long

GREETING + INTRO

_____

_____

_____

ELEMENT

_____

_____

_____

_____

_____

_____

_____

_____

CLOSING

_____

_____

_____

Tiny Talk Template
10 minutes long

GREETING + INTRO

_____

_____

_____

ELEMENT 1   ELEMENT 2   ELEMENT 3

CLOSING

_____

_____

_____

ACKNOWLEDGMENTS

This book would not exist today without the persistent and unflagging encouragement of my peer partners, Marcela Andrés and Lisa Fisher.

It wouldn't be quite so readable (or recognizably me!) but for the editorial acumen of Carla Cook.

Earliest readers Kavita Patel and Louis McQueen lovingly pointed out the sections that needed more, as well as those that needed less, and loaned me their faith when mine flagged.

We thrive in community. Angee Navarro, Anna Bryan-Borja, Autumn Keiser, Kathy Carr, Mel Abel, and Norma Fulwiler showed up for me every time I asked, and also when I was silly and didn't.

The best way to learn is to do. I am deeply honored and grateful for every single opportunity I've been offered to speak and facilitate, to co-lead beloved teams and enthusiastic audiences, whether for one week or one hour.

Finally — **especially** — to each person who has trusted me to help them with their presentation in the past 25 years: Every day I strive to be worthy of your trust and confidence. I have learned and grown so much because of you.

Thankyousomuchloveyoubye!

www.ingramcontent.com/pod-product-compliance
Lightning Source LLC
LaVergne TN
LVHW020935090426
835512LV00020B/3366